Settle to Carlisle Walk

Settle to Carlisle Walk

80 miles in sight of England's highest main-line

by
Ian & Andrew Gordon

Dalesman Books
1990

THE DALESMAN PUBLISHING COMPANY LTD.,
CLAPHAM, via Lancaster, LA2 8EB

First published 1990

ISBN: 1 85568 001 7

Printed by Peter Fretwell & Sons Ltd., Keighley, West Yorkshire BD21 1PZ

Contents

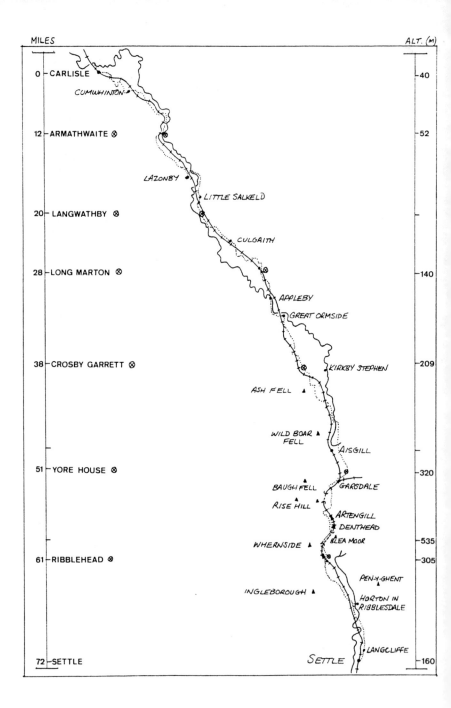

MILES

ALT. (M)

0 — CARLISLE — 40

CUMWHINTON

12 — ARMATHWAITE ⊗ — 52

LAZONBY

LITTLE SALKELD

20 — LANGWATHBY ⊗

CULGAITH

28 — LONG MARTON ⊗ — 140

APPLEBY

GREAT ORMSIDE

38 — CROSBY GARRETT ⊗ — 209

KIRKBY STEPHEN

ASH FELL ▲

WILD BOAR ▲
FELL

AISGILL

51 — YORE HOUSE ⊗ — 320

BAUGH FELL ▲

GARSDALE

RISE HILL ▲

ARTENGILL

DENTHEAD

WHERNSIDE ▲

BLEA MOOR — 535

61 — RIBBLEHEAD ⊗ — 305

PEN-Y-GHENT
▲

INGLEBOROUGH ▲

HORTON IN
RIBBLESDALE

LANGCLIFFE

72 — SETTLE

SETTLE — 160

FOREWORD

THE seeds were probably cast back in the war years of the early 1940s. I was born the son of a second generation railway man in 1943. My father, George Foster Gordon, 'Geordie' Gordon to everyone who knew him, was an employee of the London Midland and Scottish and then British Rail for 47 years. Coincidentally, so were his two brothers, John Robert and Frank, a 'Lanky man'. There was 149 years of service on the railway between them. Their father had spent 47 years before them in the same role.

The 47 years my father spent in railway service saw him start, like most, at the bottom as a cleaner on Kingmoor shed, Carlisle. Moving upwards as passed cleaner, fireman, passed fireman, driver, running foreman at Kingmoor, shed foreman at the old Canal and then at the 'Lanky', he spent the last eighteen years of his career as Locomotive Inspector based at Carlisle Citadel station. Throughout this time he worked the Settle and Carlisle. It was in the latter part of his time as a Loco inspector that he became closely involved in the return of steam engines to the S. & C., and I know well of his pride in once again riding the footplate of No.46229 *Duchess of Hamilton* over the 'Long Drag'. Not wishing to upset his many friends in the A4 Society, he loved 4498 *Sir Nigel Gresley* as well, but 'The Duchess' was a proper S. & C. locomotive. (Apologies to Julian Riddick of the A4 Society, dad's friend of many years.)

It is not surprising then that I have more than a passing interest, indeed fascination, with the Settle to Carlisle railway line.

The S. & C. is now much more than a mere route for trains and travellers. So deeply is it etched into the minds of people of the area and much father afield, that any mention, any comment, evokes instant emotion and reaction. To the outsider and railway enthusiast it is a thing of beauty, a monument to days past that must be preserved for future generations to revere. To the locals it is much more. It is their lifeline to the outside world — a living, working means of communication that has been part of their lives for more than a hundred years.

Whatever the interest, whatever the connection, the announcement in April 1989 by the Secretary of State for Transport, Paul Channon, that he was refusing an application by British Rail to close the line, signalled (excuse the pun) victory for the people who, for over five years, had waged war on British Rail in the fight to preserve this most historic of railways.

In 1987, my wife Mary and I managed a weekend's camping at Yore House not far from the Moor Cock Inn at the top end of Wensleydale. The weather was typical of upper Wensleydale, sultry rain and mist, interspersed with the occasional thunderstorm and a couple of hours of sunshine whilst the clouds gathered strength once again. The climatic conditions did not spoil our enjoyment as we walked the eastern side of Abbotside Common to Hell Gill. On approaching Hell Gill the sun managed that break through I mentioned a little earlier. The Settle and Carlisle railway line was highlighted, picking its way along the western side of Mallerstang past its summit at Ais Gill and then wending its way down into the Eden Valley towards Kirkby Stephen under the shadow of Wild Boar Fell. A Dalesrail diesel unit rattled its way up to Ais Gill on its way to Settle. I wished it had been the 'Duchess' hauling a Cumbrian Mountain Express but it was not to be.

Looking down on this scene, the thought occurred that it would be an excellent walk to trace the route of the S. & C. from its start, in Settle, over the 'Long Drag', and down the Eden Valley to Carlisle. Walking back via Ais Gill, across into Grisdale to Garsdale Head, we began to work out more detailed plans for an expedition.

Three years before, Mary and I had walked Hadrian's Wall from Wallsend on the Tyne to Bowness-on-Solway — a route following a theme of 'The Wall'. That route is now going through the process of being designated a Long Distance Path (L.D.P.). The thematic approach I believe gives added interest to the journey. We decided that we would plan for the Spring Bank holiday week in 1988, if we could have our, by then, two-and-a-half year old son William cared for by grandparents. These plans were quickly overturned by events. Backpacking 80 miles from Settle to Carlisle is not a recommended exercise for a seven-and-a-half months expectant mother. Mary and I had developed an interest in a second child which was due mid-July, only six weeks after the proposed trip.

Plans were redrawn quickly over the next few weeks. Ian Stuart, a friend of mine and an experienced walker with two Himalayan treks to his name, expressed an interest in doing the walk. Andrew, my eldest son and the co-author of this book, joined up shortly afterwards. Steve Meadows, the husband of Mary's best friend Alyson, completed the party. Mary and Alyson were to take a week's holiday together with the children in a cottage along the route to act as back-up for our every whim. The cottage, by coincidence, turned out to be a renovated ex-railway worker's cottage, built by the Midland Railway

Company and situated alongside the line at Long Marton near Appleby.

The plan we developed had four main elements; (i) to follow the route of the Settle to Carlisle as closely as possible, using established footpaths and country lanes; (ii) daily mileage to be in the region of twelve miles a day, a distance suitable for most average backpackers; (iii) the route to be flexible enough to attract a variety of different trekkers, from day excursionists using 'Dalesrail', to the 20+ miles a day 'yomper', who appears intent upon personal injury; (iv) to enjoy the experience for what it is worth and not to instigate yet another personal or collective challenge.

I also had an added objective; if this route could be created as a designated Long Distance Path (L.D.P.), a further link in the network of L.D.P.'s would be created. A walk from the estuary of the river Ribble near Preston, via the newly created 'Ribble Way', to Horton-in-Ribblesdale would intersect with either the Pennine Way or our own Settle to Carlisle. This in turn would give access to 'A walk along the Wall' (Hadrian's), which would provide a continuous pathway of approximately 200 miles between Preston in Lancashire and Wallsend-on-Tyne in Tyne and Wear by way of Carlisle in Cumbria. This in turn would assist in relieving the pressure on the premier L.D.P. in Britain, the Pennine Way. I also have a feeling that it may eventually become more popular, due to the 'theme' idea that I suggested earlier.

Readers will note that each of our days along the Settle and Carlisle starts and ends at a point aligned to a station currently offering a service to the traveller. It is quite possible to walk the route in stages, one or two days at a time, returning later to complete further stages. Additionally by using such books as *Walks from the Settle-Carlisle Railway,* by R.W. Swallow and W.R. Mitchell (Dalesman), a wider dimension of the walking possibilities in this area of Britain can be appreciated.

The important issue relating to this walk is its accessibility to the average walker. Whether you tackle the whole trip in one, or take a 'Dalesrail' to one of the stations along the line, almost anyone can take a day out, or a week out, and enjoy the history, scenic beauty and sheer stark exhilleration of Britain's most historic railway.

On foot of course!

— Ian Gordon

SETTLE TO
HORTON IN RIBBLESDALE

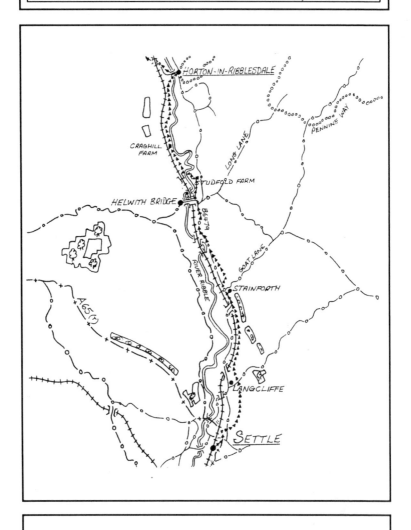

O.S. 1:25,000 Outdoor Leisure — Map 2 (The Three Peaks).
O.S. 1:50,000 Sheet 98. Wensleydale and Wharfedale.

Chapter 1

Settle to Ribblehead

"Single file it's not a motorway".

SETTLE station was alive with expectant travellers that Sunday morning, May 29th. Most were waiting for the excursion to Carlisle and the most memorable train journey in Britain. We — Ian, Andrew, Steve and myself — were anticipating just as memorable a trip along the line. They had 73 miles and perhaps just over an hour of enjoyment, with the prospect of another trip returning later in the day. We had some 80 miles, not including the gradients, and some seven days of foot-slogging before us. Still I would far rather be in my boots, excuse the pun, than their's.

After a brief inspection of Settle station, with its own simple character, and the first of the proverbial photographs, we set off on our journey. A year of thinking and planning is about to be realised. So too are three months of prediction from Ian Stuart — it begins to rain. From the time he had said he was coming along, he had been forewarning of the deplorable weather that usually accompanies his walking trips. From the Himalayas to the Munroes, rain either drizzles or thunders along with him. This day is no exception, but it does not dampen our spirits. After all, there is a long way to go, and a great deal to see and do, to let a little rain spoil our enjoyment.

Leaving the station car park, we turn into Settle town and its quite noticeable market square. In the north-east corner of the square a road takes us up and round 'Constitution Hill', where in about 250 to 300 metres it bears left, leaving us to continue on and upwards along a well-defined track towards Langcliffe. The route here is unmistakeable, at first following a green road leading to Malham, then forking left for Langcliffe marked by very good stiles for the next 3/4 of a mile.

The short trip to Langcliffe is by no means the most spectacular part of the eight-mile journey, but this first mile does help to wet the appetite for the remaining seventy-nine as we rapidly climb to over 200 metres. A wide panorama quickly opens up along Ribblesdale towards Horton in the north and westwards across the dale to Giggleswick. The line stretches back to Settle station over the first of its twenty-one viaducts, and from this vantage point on the eastern side of the dale we can see the diesel-headed excursion set off for its slow progress up the 'Long Drag' on its way to Carlisle.

The approach to Langcliffe joins the Langcliffe — Malham road only 150 metres from the village, where we turn right at the local school to locate yet another well-defined lane heading us in the direction of Stainforth. Within 300 metres, the pathway, marked unmistakeably by a sign, breaks left away from the lane to run adjacent to the railway as far as the first tunnel out of Settle, not surprisingly named 'The Stainforth Tunnel'. Before reaching the tunnel mouth one-and-a-half kilometres on, the path takes us first through a quarry yard and then past a massive kiln some 100 metres in length. This whole scene however is dominated by the towering crags of Stainforth Scar rising 150 metres above us. This must be the haunt of many a rock climber, practising for and dreaming of more established challenges in the Lakes or Scotland in days to come.

Stretching over Stainforth Tunnel we encounter our first real piece of road walking to enter Stainforth village, too early for lunch and too late for morning coffee. So, we press on, our lunch objective being Horton. We leave Stainforth via footpaths leading from a minor road known as Goat Lane which carries light traffic over to Halton Gill in Littondale, skirting Penyghent. It is a marvellous drive if you can find the time. Due to the overcast weather conditions, Penyghent is not dominating this part of Ribblesdale as yet, preferring to remain menacingly ominous in its cloud-covered shroud.

Rejoining the B6479 main road through Ribblesdale, we proceed with the road walking to the junction for Helwith Bridge some two-and-a-half kilometres further on. The weather remains dull and drizzly but not unpleasant, the coolness of the air keeping the body temperature low. At the junction on the B6479 for Helwith Bridge, we do not continue into the village, preferring to head over the open fields to Studfold by what appears to be a well-marked farm lane running directly ahead. Well-marked it might be, but easy to travel it was not. Grass reaching to the shoulders, with soft undergrowth, provides the terrain to be negotiated and it continues for some 300 metres. Emerging at the end of the lane, the pathway then takes a route across the fields to the eastern side of the Ribble, in an arc passing through a farmstead, from where it then cuts back to the riverside and a footbridge on to the western bank.

It is on this small detour that we make our first mistake. She sees us coming from a good kilometre off, and watches our approach to the farm with great interest, first from the window of the kitchen then moving out into the yard when we get closer. Trepidation begins to seep through the party in the last hundred metres, as she hovers, arms folded, awaiting our arrival.

Five metres away she speaks. "That's not the path, it's on the other side of the wall!" she states rather sternly. "Alright, I'm not going to stop you passing through," her tone softens. "I don't mind people crossing the land as long as they use the path," she adds, then pausing, ". . . but don't forget it's not a motorway, get in single file."

I do wish I had asked her name because she was really a nice lady who was only interested in seeing that the rules of the countryside were followed. Indeed, having explained our mission to walk to Carlisle along the route of the railway, she warmed most noticeably, and we part with a few helpful words of assistance as to the direction of travel to find the footbridge crossing the Ribble to the western bank. For the rest of the journey her words are constantly with us whenever straying feet step out of line "Single file, it's not a motorway!" is the refrain.

Crossing the footbridge, we find the most pleasant walking to date, if we ignore the drastic scarring caused by the quarrying operations, as the pathway follows the river bank to the north. Sunday afternoon strollers or trekkers would both find this walk to their liking, even in the rain which is now falling heavily. Noah Stuart smiles serenely.

With the railway only a few metres to the right and the river a few to the left, we progress past Craghill Farm and Garth House, eventually arriving in Horton in Ribblesdale at a little before one o'clock. Lunch consists of lasagne, and two or three pints of 'Theakston's reviver' to wash it down, in the New Inn. We are to meet the 'support team' here as they return from recovering our early morning transport from Settle station. As there is no sign of Mary, Alyson and the kids, another pint of Theakston's seems the best way of calming our fears for their well-being. They finally arrive, looking somewhat hassled after spending almost two hours on a journey down from Long Marton, having to contend with the three children. Still, it is good to see them.

Setting out from Horton, well-nourished, some would say

HORTON IN RIBBLESDALE
TO RIBBLEHEAD

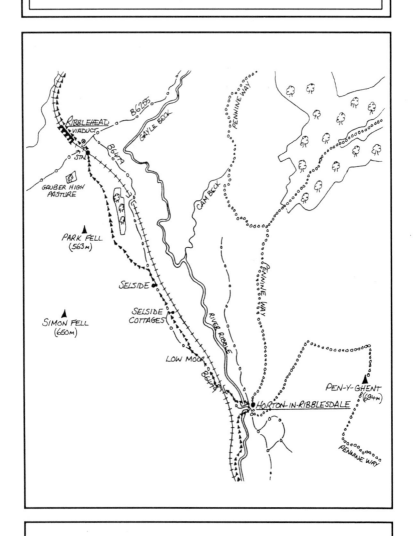

O.S. 1:25,000 Outdoor Leisure — Map 2

oiled, we head for Selside. A short walk across a field path brings us to Rowe Farm where we join the main road for approximately one-and-a-half kilometres to Low Moor, where a footpath, well signposted, breaks right across country to Selside cottages. The weather has turned for the better now and the sun begins to shine, the clouds are lifting from Penyghent and it all fares well for tomorrow. Indeed, we only see rain once more during walking time until the following Saturday. Mind, it fairly chucks it down at night time when we are trying to sleep.

With the good assistance of sunshine, the dale is now being seen at its best. The distinctive lines of Penyghent, now well clear of cloud and bathed in blue sky, descend to the greens and browns of the lower valley where the river Ribble wends its leisurely way towards Preston and the sea. Other people might care to extol the virtues of the Lakes or Scotland for their stark but majestic scenery. For me, the rolling fells of the Dales and the more spacious bottom land excude an atmosphere of peacefulness and harmony that is missing from these other places of more popular attraction.

Stripped of the 'wet-gear', the walking now becomes almost leisurely cutting across country towards Selside cottages. These cottages, identical to those already seen at Ellwood near Langcliffe, and to those that Mary, Alyson and the children are staying in at Long Marton, are a regular feature of the journey. The group of twelve built at Selside are the largest group, outside of major junctions such as Hawes and Carlisle, along the whole line. In almost every case one is struck by the sheer remoteness of the position and thoughts of those people living in them, in the real 'age of the train'. Signalmen, crossing keepers, permanent way staff, porters, clerical staff and the elitist station master — all were provided for by the Midland Railway Company in its construction of the railway. In all, 149 cottages were built for company employees, many of which are in continued occupation, in varying states of repair and tenure.

Immediately on passing Selside cottages, we return to road walking for one-and-a-half kilometres as we pass through the village of Selside, a small but attractive hamlet within 100 metres of the line. Five hundred metres out of the village a track, well signed, leaves the road to the west and upwards, skirting Park Fell (563m) in a northerly direction to Colt Park, via Bent Hill Rigg. Look for a remarkable landmark here, a monstrous rock, squatting in the field like some gigantic toad awaiting its lunch.

As we have progressed the weather has improved dramatically and along with it the view. To the fore and slightly to the west, the slopes of Park Fell give way to the looming hulk of Whernside across the vale of Batty Moss. To the north-east are Widdale and Dodd Fell (668m), below which on the Cam High Road the Pennine Way and Dales Way meet and then wend their separate ways to the north and west. Over our shoulders, to the south-east, Penyghent is beginning to recede into the distance, but still remains so distinct with its slipped saddle shape clearly defined. This whole panorama is enhanced even more as we traverse the limestone pavement over Gauber High Pasture to our first glimpse of Ribblehead Viaduct, at this distance nestling in the dale bottom some one-and-a-half kilometres away.

Soon we reach Ribblehead station, where a lone passenger, half sitting, half lying, wiles away the time waiting for the next train to Settle. He does not seem to mind that its arrival time is 6.50pm and it is only 4.05. Ribblehead retains that strange welcoming feeling that stations often have. I feel it must be because they suggest a population centre, and are as much about coming home as they are about going away.

Leaving the station by its old approach road, we quickly come on to the B6255 Hawes to Ingleton road at the Station Inn. This is to be our first overnight camp, by chance in the close vicinity of a friendly hostelry, where we can be spared the spartan delicacies of camp food for the warm welcome of good pub food and its attendant nectar.

The area between here and Sandy Hill, just across the junction of the B6255 and the B6479 Ribblehead to Horton road, is a mass of holiday and weekend trippers. Cars, infernal motorbikes, cycles and walkers are in abundance, all intent upon enjoying the sun and air of the head of the dale. Unfortunately some are also intent on spoiling the enjoyment of others, with their escapades through crowded areas on thundering machines, or filling the air with 120 decibels of pop music from 'ghetto blasters' that could be heard back in Settle.

After rejecting a campsite on the bank side of the stream, in case it should come on heavy rain in the night and flood the tents, we settled for nice grassy bank immediately behind the Station Inn. Looking forward to dinner we all take a short nap for an hour or two, which does a lot to rest our not too weary legs and feet after our first day on the road. Dinner and a pint or four of the local Theakston's repairs the other part of the suffering anatomy, the stomach, before we bed down for the night. The night air is cool, but the alcohol warming on leaving the inn, so we decide on a supper time drink of hot soup under the clearing sky.

In these days of outdoor pursuits, when people not only walk the Three Peaks but run, jog and even cycle them, I suppose I should not have been so surprised. Imagine the feeling of consternation, not to mention sheer disbelief, spreading rapidly through our slightly inebriated band when out of the gloom of Whernside, up the slope from Batty Moss bottom, comes a traveller of a different kind. Wearing a caver's hard hat with a lantern attached is a gentleman, riding at some rate of knots, a 'pogo-stick'. Talk about 'pink elephants'! I expected to see many rare sights on this walk, but never one so bizarre as this. We are unlucky, in that our camera equipment is stowed safely away for the night, and thus are unable to produce conclusive evidence of this outlandish event. Hopefully, some day the itinerant Three Peaks 'pogo-sticker' will be revealed.

Ribblehead Station

17

The Legend of Batty Moss

The end of May, 1888,
A ganger on line did meet his fate,
The night express was charging, full of steam
From the depths of Blea Moor, like a Devil's dream.

His lantern alight, he jumped the line,
The driver oblivious couldn't stop in time,
The light went out, no cries of pain,
For a century later, He'd roam again.

Four packers walking, from Settle to Carlisle,
Pitched camp, not far, upon the twelfth mile,
The billy cans boiling, the soup and the bread,
A ghostly legend had rose from the dead.

The night drew in an eerie smell,
We turned our gaze up Whernside Fell,
A light did flicker, and caught our eye,
No farm, no house, built up on high.

No car, no cycle, the light did march,
From Ribblehead Viaduct's seventh arch,
Was this vision, the mist playing a trick?
No, 'twas the Batty Moss Phantom on a pogo stick.

The ghoul bounced closer, through grass and mud,
No face could be seen, beneath the black hood,
We stood in amazement, as away he went,
And vanished into the night, toward Peny-y-Ghent.

RIBBLEHEAD TO
COW DUB BRIDGE

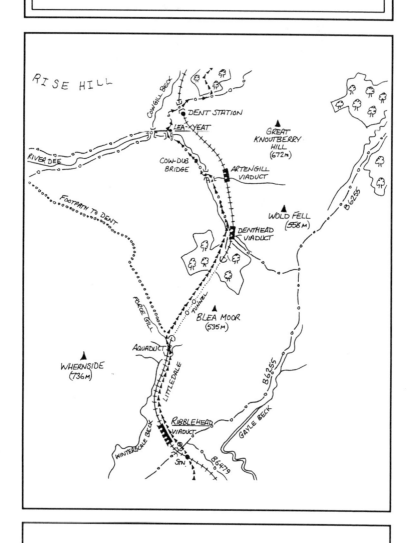

O.S. 1:25,000 Outdoor Leisure — Map 2

Chapter 2

Ribblehead to Moor Cock Inn

"Skinned heels and twisted ankles"

WAKING to the sound of the early morning train from Carlisle, as it trundles carefully over Ribblehead viaduct into Ribblehead station, is one of the pleasures in life of which, until now, I have been sorely unaware. I hope it will be one that I shall experience again in the future.

Lying there in the damp cool of the morning, reflecting upon the previous day's journey, and eagerly anticipating the day ahead, it is so easy to forget the wider world outside. Easy that is, until the heavy rumble of Andrew's snoring, two feet away, brings one quickly down to earth. Rain has fallen heavily overnight, the sky is grey and angry, yet a single ray of sunlight is picking out the 24 arches of the viaduct in a haunting sort of way. The grey clouds, rolling down off Whernside, then quickly envelop the ray, leaving the great stone monument in the sinister hovering gloom.

Breakfast of bacon and eggs sets us up for the day. Clearing the site of our first night halt creates an eagerness to be away again, this time in the hope of a fine day's hike over the most exciting part of the route. We are once again not to be disappointed.

By the time of leaving, the cloud has begun to lift and the prospect of a fine day is less remote. We cut across the moor, alongside the path on which the midnight pogo-sticker had come galloping towards us the previous night. The arches of the viaduct tower over us as we follow the path of so many 'Three Peaks' walkers on their way up Whernside. The well-defined route is now so eroded that it has had to be reinforced with a hard core rock to give it a base. The path wends its way alongside the railway for nearly two kilometres to Blea Moor signal box. Is it my imagination or are there a pair of hiker's boots resting in the window? If so, they look rather battered, as if having done a hundred rounds of the 'Three Peaks'.

Here we again see the wide variety of methods of transport that travellers are prepared to use in order to traverse the Three Peaks round. Last night a 'pogo-stick'; this morning, mountain bikes. A couple of people seem to be enjoying the variation on a theme as they descend the north edge of Whernside with screams of glee. Or is it trepidation? I feel sure the only form of conveyance that could not be tried with any measure of success must be roller skates, or perhaps the skate board. But, only then, due to the sticky morass of the footpath and not the endeavour of the traveller.

The signal box at Blea Moor stands adjacent to Blea Moor siding, at which spot in 1952 the most famous of Midland route trains, the Thames-Clyde Express, was derailed. Miraculously no one was killed, injuries being noted as a little over thirty to both passengers and crew from a total of around 200 people on the train.

At this point, Blea Moor really begins to justify its reputation for bleak wilderness of terrain. Although now towards the end of May, the early morning, whilst attempting to allow the sun to break out, still threatens to turn into dark and thundery night as cloud rolls down from Whernside enveloping the group in dampening mist and drizzle. What must the place have been like in mid-winter, building bridges, digging tunnels and laying rails?

Leaving Blea Moor box behind, we continue along the path on the northern side of the line along Blue Clay Ridge as far as the aqueduct and its neighbouring bridge, just short of the southern entrance to Blea Moor Tunnel. If Ribblehead Viaduct provides the greatest monument to the bridge-building railway engineer of the 19th century, then surely this tunnel must do likewise for the tunneller. Some 2.7 kilometres in length, it carries the line to a little over 137 metres below the moor before emerging into upper Dentdale.

Pausing for a while on this bridge overlooking Blea Moor Tunnel allows us to take in more of the features of this part of the moor, which is in fact Little Dale. Just over the bridge wall, on the southern side, is the aqueduct carrying Force Gill over the line to merge with Little Beck. Constructed of stone blocks, double bends sweep the waters of the stream over the line with such precision that is it easy to conclude the water bridge gradually evolved with the surrounding landscape, rather than being built by stonemasons only a century ago.

The panoramic view from this point is worthy of a trip all of its own. To the north the line of the tunnel is defined by the footpath that rises steeply over Blea Moor, between the twin mounds of spoil remaining from the building operations.

Blea Moor Tunnel — south end

Off to the north-east, via Force Gill, is the well-established green road which takes the traveller to Dent village, some eight kilometres distant, along the Craven Way. To the south the bonus — the view down Little Dale, in the rapidly developing light is something to behold. The converging twin lines of rail draw the eye to the distant flat-topped hump of Ingleborough like a magnet. With its two slipped saddles picked out in the improving sunlight, Ingleborough dominates the surrounding landscape.

Continuing, we eventually cross the bridge, and immediately leave the Dent road to climb over the portal of the tunnel, to follow the path that is directly over the line of the tunnel for the next 2.4 kilometres. The direction is now a little to the east of north, and the terrain climbing steeply over the moor. Guidelines are clearly marked by the spoil heaps, mentioned earlier, some half way up the climb. On approaching the heaps, one of the original air shafts for the tunnel can be seen. Passing the second group of spoil heaps, the climb slackens to a gentle rise as the path reaches 500 metres (1,640 ft) only 35 metres from the summit of Blea Moor, before starting its descent into Dentdale.

On reaching the summit we take time out for a rest, the scenery so excelling itself that it becomes nearly indescribable. For ten minutes past the sun has begun to shine, highlighting every feature of the view. Looking down on upper Dentdale is sheer delight, with innumerable shades of green carpeting the valley. The River Dee fleetingly sparkles into view as it meanders its way northwards, soon to turn west to the village of Dent. And the line; it clings to the hillside like a limpet, as it emerges from the northern portal of the tunnel. First over Denthead Viaduct, then over Arten Gill, it precariously continues its passage along the western slopes of Wold Fell, then Dent Fell and finally Great Knoutberry Hill, before arriving at Dent.

The descent from Blea Moor proceeds through the middle of a fire-break in a forestry plantation directly on to the northern mouth of the tunnel. The footpath then leaves the line to descend into the dale via Dent Head Farm, Bridge End Cottage and the minor road in the valley bottom leading to Dent. Before pressing on we find time to take-in the waterfalls, the footbridge over the Dee and, by deviating slightly, the majestic span of Denthead Viaduct as it reaches across firstly Fell End gill and then the valley bottom road. It is of little surprise on this holiday Monday to find some ten or more cars surrounding this place, their occupants having travelled here just to enjoy the scene.

It was always our intention when preparing this walk to avoid road walking at all costs. This quite obviously is impossible, but still we tried. The next five kilometres is 'on the road' but far from unpleasant. With the sun now streaming down, the walk down from Denthead through the shade of overhanging trees is most enjoyable. The thought of some early refreshment at the Sportsman inn, Cow Dubb, gives added incentive to the pace. Just past the Youth Hostel at Mount Pleasant, approaching the house named 'Scow', we come across a novel residence. In a small 'GR' post box, attached to a fence post, a small bird has made its home for the spring. Attached to the box is a note which reads, 'Bird Nesting in Letter Box . . . Please do not post letters'. Quite obviously the birds in Dentdale are a much more intelligent species than elsewhere.

Pressing on we pass Arten Gill viaduct with its 36 metre arches stretching high over Arten Gill Beck, which divides Wold Fell (558m) from one of the Dale's notable peaks, Great Knoutberry Hill (672m). The viaduct is a further fine example of the engineering skills of the Victorian railway engineer, overcoming immense difficulties of terrain and climate to create a structure that appears at one with environment. Leaving Arten Gill behind we quickly arrive at the Sportsman. Not a moment too soon for some. The first complaints of sore feet and aching shoulders begin to come from the group.

The bar meal is excellent and the liquid Theakston's even more welcome. After lunch the effort to pick up the packs once again and walk is somewhat strained, as is, come to mention it, my right ankle. Having sat for a time, each one of us finds re-oiling the joints and re-starting the muscles something of a trial. Eventually movement returns and we set off on the remaining kilometre of the walk along Dentdale bottom. It is with some reluctance we do so, as a detour to the picturesque village of Dent would be an excellent afternoon's excursion.

At the road junction at Lea Yeat bridge, we turn right up along the road that leads to Dent station and over to Garsdale, known as the 'Coal Road'. How people from Dent ever contemplated using the railway as a means of transport from the dale is beyond my comprehension. Within a distance of just over a kilometre, the road rises 130 metres (426ft) to the station. Apart from this startling drawback to travelling convenience,

COW DUB BRIDGE TO
MOOR COCK INN

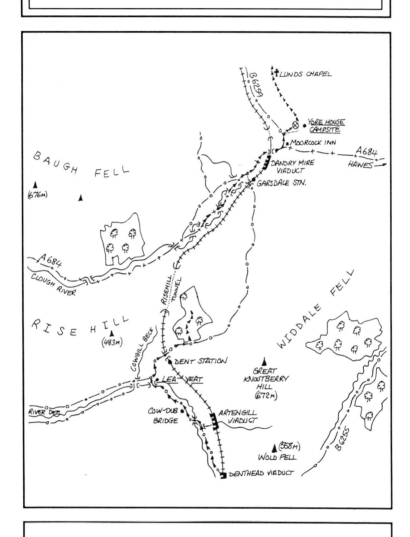

O.S. 1:25,000 Outdoor Leisure — Map

one must add that the village of Dent, which the station purports to serve, is approximately eight kilometres away. In winter the station can be closed due to heavy snowfall; in 1947 this was for a period of no less than eight weeks, with only the occasional snow plough breaking through to bring respite. Dent station is no mean railway halt. It is the highest main-line station in Britain at 352 metres (1,155ft) above sea level. Now in private hands, the platforms give access only to bona-fide travellers.

From this point we have an even more breathtaking panorama. In bright sunlight, the view to the south picks out the line as it passes over first Arten Gill and then Denthead Viaducts before being swallowed by the northern mouth of Blea Moor Tunnel. To the west the widening dale of Dent, in glorious shades of green, lies basking in the springtime sun. This one moment makes all the work, all the preparation, all the pain from the now worsening ankle, a hundred times worthwhile.

After resting for some time at this point we move on upwards, still moaning about the gradient. At the gateway to the Forestry Commission land, on the left 600 metres further, we take a detour through the forest. Normally forest walking tends to be most uninteresting, but here the roadway is wide, if extremely uneven, allowing the eye to see further than the next conifer. Progress is rapid, if a bit undulating. Following the main path we emerge, some forty minutes later, at the forest edge overlooking Garsdale and Risehill Tunnel, some 60 metres above the line.

Here we are faced with a dilemma. For the first time we do not have a recognised footpath to follow. Hopefully, if this walk eventually becomes a Long Distance Footpath (L.D.P.), an agreement can be reached between the Forestry Commission, British Rail and the landowners for a public right-of-way from the edge of the woodland, along the railway boundary to the bridge above Low Scar, and thence down to the A684 via a suitable field footpath. The route through the forest takes one some distance away from the line and its second longest tunnel. No less exposed than Blea Moor, Rise Hill Tunnel caused just the same type of problems to the engineers. It would be a significant contribution to the interested trekker if the sort of access there is over Blea Moor was also available over Rise Hill. Not only would it make it simpler to see the tunnel but it would resolve many of the problems of navigating this particular area of the route. For the moment, there is no legal alternative but to return through the forest and follow the

Coal Road over to Garsdale station.

On reaching the A684 Hawes-Sedbergh road through Garsdale we turn due east for the Moor Cock. Being late in the day and with the ankle giving real pain now, road walking is even more of a bind. Not until we approach the last kilometre does anything on the line produce a murmur of interest. The murmurings are caused by the Dandry Mire Viaduct, which has special significance in the building of the line as at the planning stage it was not envisaged. After three years of attempting to fill in the area with ballast to create an embankment, only to see their efforts come to nought as the broken stone sank steadily into the oozing bog of peat, the engineers recommended that the only possible solution to the problem was a viaduct. This was eventually constructed, creating a further major outlay of capital by the Midland Railway Company and much dismay for the engineers.

Passing under the arch of the Moor Cock bridge, only 200 metres west of the Moor Cock Inn, thoughts develop of an early kip but even more of food. But first, to lay down a base. We pitch at Yore House Farm, some 800 metres from the inn. Having established a base we immediately 'crash out' (retire) for a couple of hours. I wake, Andrew doesn't, to find the tent awash below. The thunderstorm that fails to wake us takes its toll, surface water flooding under the groundsheet on its way to the raging River Ure. We are camped in the headland of the main waterway of Wensleydale. After moving the tent to more suitable ground, drenched to the skin with the late rainstorm, we decide to seek solace in the comforting warmth of the Moor Cock Inn. Here we dine and sup in plenty to ease our aching bones and minds.

It's a dark walk back from the Moor Cock to Yore House. I should know, I've done it twice before. When the moon is up it's very pleasant. Tonight, unfortunately, it isn't. Throughout the day the ankle has been steadily getting worse and I fear its condition in the morning. The only remedy available seems to be a good soak in the flooding River Ure. Sitting on the river bank at half eleven at night is extremely restful, and for fifteen minutes or so I steep my feet in the ice cold water, listening to the rushing torrent of the Ure as it floods over the falls at Yore House Farm.

Today has proved the most memorable day of the walk. Whilst all the other days produce excellent walking in ideal surroundings, places of interest and good company, this Monday over Blea

Moor into Dentdale will always be remembered as something special. We even manage to purchase, from the landlord of the Moor Cock Inn, bacon, sausage and eggs for the morrow. We rest easy that night in full knowledge of the cooked breakfast to come at first light.

Dent Station and Upper Dentdale

MOOR COCK INN TO
DEEP GILL

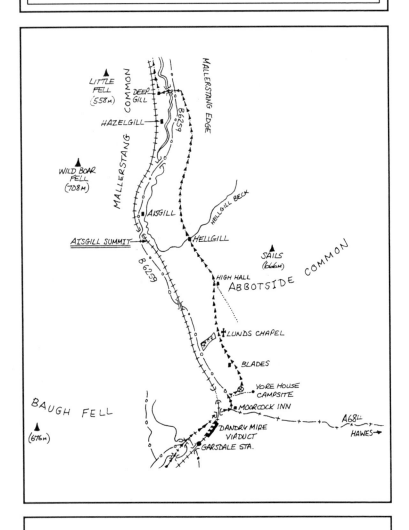

O.S. 1:50,000 Sheet 98. Wensleydale and Wharfedale.
O.S. 1:50,000 Sheet 91. Appleby-in-Westmorland.

Chapter 3

Moor Cock Inn to Crosby Garrett

"Mash and fish."

A DAMP, dank, miserable gloom pervades the air around Mallerstang Common on Tuesday morning, the 31st May, as I poke a none too eager nose out of the 'Peapod' door to test the weather conditions for the day. Heavy overnight rain has brought the Ure into full spate and the waterfall teams a cascade of white water, with a thundering roar through the bridge and over the fall. A more spectacular start to the day you could not wish for.

A quick wash and brush up precedes a much longer soak of the feet in the raging ure. Breakfast of bacon, sausage (best Cumberland, is it Robson's?) and eggs, the fare of our landlord of the previous evening, is devoured with consummate ease. There is nothing quite like a fry-up over the camp stove in the early morning, wet or dry, followed by 'mashings' of tea. So much is the meal enjoyed by all that thoughts of tomorrow's breakfast are aroused 24 hours early. Will we be able to acquire similar rations along today's route over Mallerstang to Crosby Garrett? For the first time concern is expressed as to our future dietary provision and stores. A little late I feel, but not to worry, from the depths of Ian's rucksack appears an air-tight silver-foil pack labelled 'Mash and Fish'! Ian says, "It tastes horrible, but you'll eat it if you're hungry." He then continues by telling us all how horrible before returning the package to his sack. Thoughts of the possibility of having to partake of this food haunt us for the rest of the trip and various schemes are developed, most of them unmentionable here, as to how we might dispose of the sinister package without hurting Ian's feelings.

During breakfast we chat over the day's trip and the possible difficulties due to heavy packs and the injuries that occurred the previous day. Steve and Andrew complain of sore shoulders, I moan on about my ankle, whilst Ian, we are to find out later in the day, is nursing the biggest blister I or we have ever seen. Due to an ill-fitting boot, his right heel from top to bottom is completely devoid of skin. How he manages to get through the day without even the slightest mumble I do not know. His only comment later is to be, "I should have known, it happened the last time I wore these particular boots." To tell the truth, he didn't in fact say particular.

At this moment, the partial solution to our troubles arrives. Like the Seventh Cavalry in those John Wayne westerns, Mary and William in one car and Alyson, Kate and David in another come over the hill and down the lane. The relief of Mafeking cannot have been greeted with more delight than the sight of the back-up team coming to our rescue. We stow our packs into the boot of each car, for their transportation to our next halt in Crosby Garrett. Complicated instructions for their deposit at (i) the Post Office, (ii) the police station or (iii) the prominent house in the village (public) are relayed and the 'back-up' team leaves for its destination. This routine proves so successful that it is adopted for the remaining days of the walk, with only a small day pack, cameras and navigation equipment being carried by ourselves.

Setting out from Yore House Farm site, we take a path to the left immediately on crossing the bridge over the Ure. The track is quite well worn and heads in a northerly direction towards a hamlet named Blades and on to the derelict chapel at Lunds. Our plan is to follow the path to Hell Gill, and then pass along Mallerstang Common, before dropping down to cross the River Eden at Deep Gill.

It is as well to mention that there is an equally adequate alternative route that trekkers may wish to take. This follows the line on the western side of Mallerstang to Ais Gill Summit, then along the banks of the Eden to reconnect with the first route at Deep Gill. Ais Gill Summit is the highest point on the line at 356 metres (1,169ft), so perhaps some will prefer this alternative, which is described in more detail later.

The ground underfoot is extremely wet and muddy from the heavy overnight rain, but does not deter progress over the low moorland of Abbotside Common, and we quickly reach Blades. Originally a farmstead it is now converted, in part, into a restaurant. Our next objective, the chapel at Lunds, is reached by passing through the farmyard at Blades. At the gate on the far side, turn sharp left in a northerly direction and follow the footpath to Lunds. The first marker, if still there, is a derelict caravan lying in the field side; the second, a lone telegraph pole on top of the rise immediately to the fore. Passing over the rise, we descend to cross the Ure in the dale bottom. The pathway again rises directly over a small hill where, with close inspection, a stile can be seen cutting through the field wall. We head over marshy ground to the stile, and from there over the point of the hill.

On reaching the crest of the hill, Lunds chapel can be seen nestling in the dale bottom, close to the farm house of Beck Side. It is difficult to imagine this small chapel in such a remote site ever being filled with worshippers at Sunday services. It is said that some of the railway navvies were buried here during the construction of the line, but the remaining headstones are so eroded that it is difficult to identify any of them. We dwelt a while in this quiet churchyard, absorbing some of the peacefulness of the scene.

Pushing on through Beck Side, some 200 to 300 metres on, we take the right fork in the path and head upwards to High Hall and Mallerstang Common. High Hall, now a derelict set of buildings which in the past must have dominated this part of the daleside, is set beside the downfall of Washer Gill. The only means of access for vehicles to this farmstead is by the bridlepath known as High Way, which fords Washer Gill at this point, or directly up the hillside through the fields below. Either way, it is not the terrain for anything less than a tractor or just possibly a Land Rover.

Going on from High Hall we cross the ford over Washer Gill and follow the footpath north towards Hell Gill. As the sun breaks from behind the clouds a pleasant warmth spreads over the moorland. The path for the next 500 metres is deeply rutted by vehicle tracks but not too difficult to navigate. We then come on to an area of moorland with the occasional outcrop of limestone, which continues to the gate and bridge over Hell Gill.

Hell Gill Beck is the source of the River Eden, the only river of note in Britain which flows from south to north for the majority of its course. Some seventy miles plus in length, the Eden travels from this point on the Cumbria and North Yorkshire border northwards to the Solway Firth. Hell Gill itself is a dramatic site at this point of crossing. With care it is just possible, by leaning over the bridge parapet and peering into the seemingly bottomless gorge of the Gill, to detect the water many metres below. A little further down the hillside Hell Gill drops over a beautiful fall, then turns north, joining with Far Cote Gill to form the Eden.

This point is also a most advantageous position for viewing

DEEP GILL TO
CROSBY GARRETT

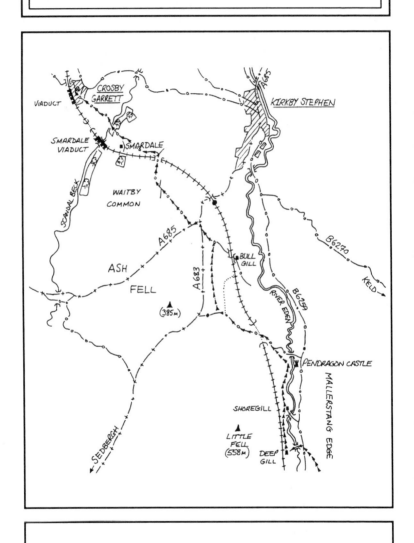

O.S. 1:50,000 Sheet 91. Appleby-in-Westmorland.

Ais Gill Summit, which lies some 300 to 400 metres inside the North Yorkshire border in a cutting just south of Ais Gill Cottages. In the push to reach the summit of the 'Long Drag', from Carlisle in the north or from Settle in the south, many a locomotive fireman's spirit, if not his heart, has been broken. Wherever railwaymen tell their tales, the drive for Ais Gill summit will feature in their stories. My father tells of the inspector who, not to show weakness in the sight of adversity, left the footplate in the winter of 1981 to communicate with hard-pressed permanent way staff who were trying to maintain a clear line, and immediately found himself unable to move, up to his armpits in snow, ('I told you so'). And the time, in the winter of 1947, when as a fireman he had to climb on top of the tender, to push off bales of straw that the engine crew had been asked to get to the stricken farmers of Mallerstang. The bales were then delivered to anxious waiting mouths by the momentum of crashing down the dale side. But if one episode tells of the feelings of railwaymen toward this particular spot then the following should serve to illustrate the fact. My father's closest colleague in his years as locomotive inspector, Mr. Joe Armstrong, died not long after his retirement from B.R. His ashes are now scattered over the line at Ais Gill.

Moving on from Hell Gill we continue along the very pronounced bridlepath that skirts the slope of Mallerstang Common for the next two kilometres before descending to the Eden Valley bottom at Deep Gill. Before making the descent we are overtaken by a party of riders on horseback who are pony-trekking in the area. We know this, as we met the same party, two days before, at our lunch time stop in Horton-in-Ribblesdale. The ground is very easy up here. The bridlepath is some six metres wide and would do justice to the wicket at Lord's, such is the quality of the short rich turf underfoot.

That said, the ground beneath on the drop to the dale bottom is most uneven and deeply rutted. By now the pain from the ankle is only just bearable, and it is with great relief that we make our lunchtime halt, on the river bank beside the bridge over the Eden, where Deep Gill joins the main stream. The troops are not too pleased, on planning grounds, as a pub and the thirst-quenching Theakston's are not within reach. Yet the cursing is nothing to that to be found later in Crosby Garrett. The substitute of a good soak of the feet in the Eden does not appear sufficient compensation for the sulking deprived. The soaking of the ankle in the cold waters of the Eden reduces the swelling and eases the discomfort.

After lunching on sandwiches, provided earlier by Mary and Alyson, we move off up the made-up track, westward toward the line, in order to re-establish our close connection with the focal point of the journey. On reaching the line fence, we turn right on a northerly tack and proceed to Sycamore Farm. From there we drop down to follow the west bank of the Eden to Pendragon Castle. This broken ruin is purportedly the ancient seat of the father of King Arthur. Derelict it may be in the twentieth century, but it is easy to perceive its importance, centuries before, as it is strategically positioned, overlooking the junction of three roads, a river and a bridge. He who controlled this castle controlled the movement of people or goods to and from all points of the compass.

Leaving Pendragon Castle we follow the footpath away from the river to the farms close-by, where we join the farm tracks which take us to the minor road that passes over Birkett Tunnel and around the northern face of Wharton Fell. From this time on to the end of the day, I wish I had never seen a pair of walking boots, a rucksack or a tent in my life. The soothing effect of the bathing of the ankle in the Eden has now worn off and the lack of any preparatory training for the walk begins to take its revenge. The next two and a half hours are sheer agony, as every step of the right foot shoots arrows of seering pain from the ankle to the hip. Still, the only solution is to press on, which we do. On breasting the rise over Wharton Fell, the A683 Kirkby Stephen to Sedbergh road can be seen on the hillside across the moor. Lorries and cars pass with monotonous regularity, heralding our return to the wider civilisation where many people think that to travel any distance by placing one foot in front of another is crass stupidity. I often reflect upon this attitude as I watch with interest one after the other motorist attempting to find parking space alongside the cash-out till in the local supermarket. Stupidity?

We leave the minor road over Wharton Fell to take the footpath on the right that leads directly to Wharton Dikes. The ground is flat and quite even, giving a good footing for nearly two kilometres. On reflection, a more suitable alternative would have been the path through Greengate, Bullgill and then Wharton Dikes, but we can all be cleverer after the event. From here it is only a short distance along the minor country lane to the major road junction of the A683 and the A685 Kirkby Stephen to Tebay road, near Basegill Head. At this junction we turn west for 100 metres to the next turning on the right which is the minor road to Waitby, over Waitby Common. Road walking is not to be recommended, but these are pleasant country lanes and the sun is shining brightly. It has been my concern from the outset that some disinterest would set in after we left behind the wilder parts of the trek. This concern is proved quite wrong as for the next few days we are to enjoy the much different but no less beautiful terrain of the Eden Valley as it wends its way through to Carlisle and the Solway.

Passing over Waitby Common we pass by the first turning on the right for Waitby, and continue along the lane further, where it then bears sharply to the right and drops, passing under the line, to meet the Waitby to Smardale road within a matter of metres. At this junction we turn left towards Smardale and on towards Crosby Garrett. Within a kilometre we meet a further junction and bear left once again. The now dismantled North Eastern Railway from Darlington to Tebay (closed in 1962) runs adjacent to this junction and then under the 40 metres (130ft) Smardale Viaduct, the highest along the Settle to Carlisle. With twelve spans and 216 metres long, Smardale is second only to the gigantic Ribblehead of the viaducts on the line. In addition to the N.E.R. it also straddles Scandal Beck, a tributary of the Eden which has its source up on the western side of Wild Boar Fell. We cross over Scandal Beck by the ford 400 metres below the viaduct, then follow the same road uphill on the approach to Crosby Garrett.

The church at Crosby Garrett is an impressive sight, standing guard like some great stone sentinel, perched on the high ground to the north of the village. The last two hundred metres seem like two thousand, but isn't that always the case. Into the village and on to the green, anxious eyes casting quickly around in every direction, searching . . . ? The village is dry! Howls of derision from the rest of the party descend on myself. What manner of planning is it that not only fails to provide a lunch-time watering hole, but also a place to spend the darkening evening with a warming pint or four? Withdrawal symptoms spread quickly over the eyes of the three.

After the shock has subsided, we determine to act more sensibly and find where the rucksacks have been deposited earlier in the day by the backup team. There's no pub or police station, but there is a post office — well, a sort of post office. In the centre of the village, set back off the road to the eastern side of the green with a lovely piece of lawn out front, is a house. To the rear of the house is the post office, situated in an outhouse of the main building. The post-mistress is a cheery country woman, ready to help and advise, but has not seen or heard of our packs. After purchasing some supplies of food, fruit and soft drinks, we park our bodies outside on the lawn. Andrew immediately drops into his usual deep sleep, whilst the rest of us doze in the afternoon sun. half an hour later we are ready to return to the search for the packs. A young man, who we find out is a B.R. worker on the permanent way staff, tells us that he has seen a number of rucksacks left outside a house at the top end of the village, just below Crosby Garret Viaduct. He also goes off to see a farmer to ask if it is alright to pitch our tents in the field behind the farm, to which the farmer readily agrees.

After pitching camp and a further rest, thoughts begin to turn to our stomachs. The dreaded thought of settling our starvation by indulging in Ian's compressed pack of 'Mash 'n Fish' stirs me into action. A taxi to Kirkby Stephen! A short walk to the phone box, strategically placed at the field gate, quickly disabuses us of the idea. £16 return! On returning to the camp I find Ian and Andrew chatting to a local chap, Ian Allonby. It transpires that Ian is a member of the Friends of the Settle to Carlisle Line, an action group dedicated to preserving the route as a proper working railway, serving the community of Ribblesdale and the Eden Valley. He shows some interest in our expedition and we quickly strike up an acquaintance. Ian then takes charge of all our dining arrangements for the evening by firstly transporting us to Kirkby Stephen, a distance of some four miles, and then returning at 10.30 pm to transport us back to Crosby Garrett. He then invites us into his home, a railway cottage adjacent to the line, to provide late night coffee and intense chat lasting until the early hours. This impromptu act of good neighbourliness and genuine goodwill is all too lacking in town life nowadays, yet wherever we go in the countryside on this trip we find time and again people only too willing to come to our assistance. We retire that night with a great sense of comfort from meeting the people of Crosby Garrett.

Chapter 4

Crosby Garrett to Long Marton

"Derby day bath."

SUN streams down over our little camp on the morning of Wednesday, June 1st. The air is crisp and clean and smells of the late spring and early summer. It is Derby Day. I am sure I know the winner of the best-known of all English horse races, so we need to be in Appleby by 3.00 pm if I am to place the winning bet.

Our reception in Crosby Garrett has been superb, and I am to have breakfast with Ian Allonby at 7.30. I leave the other three still dead to the world. The raucous snoring of Andrew is the only suggestion that there is life after death. For the first time on the trip I am to be treated to the luxury of a prepared breakfast; until now I appear to be the self-elected chief cook and bottle washer. Today I have it easy. Ian Allonby and I spend a jaw-jaw hour or more over toast, marmalade and endless cups of coffee, discussing the walk, the line and a multitude of other inter-related topics. We are eventually interrupted by Andrew and Steve, who appear to be finding difficulty in how to wash dishes. Ian mentions that water is a useful medium, preferably hot, and points to the sink. It appears that Andrew has found a new method of cleaning those really messy 'billies', the ones that have crisp, brown remains of scrambled egg welded to the bottom. You just heat the beans in the same pan and, like magic, the egg remains are removed to add flavour to the beans.

The one problem with homely welcomes is that you do not want to leave when the time comes, but needs must. Returning to the trek is not easy, but we say our goodbyes and stroll out of Crosby Garrett, the sun now beating down. We are late — it is 10.45 am. Heading north out of the village we bear left at the fork, just below the church, and head toward Gallansay. After a little over a kilometre on the country lane we pass under the line, and quickly reach a junction with the Soulby-Great Asby road. At the junction we turn left and within a few metres right again. After 700 metres we pass over the line and pause for a few moments to take in the air and negotiate the route. Immediately upon crossing the bridge, we take a

CROSBY GARRETT TO
GREAT ORMSIDE

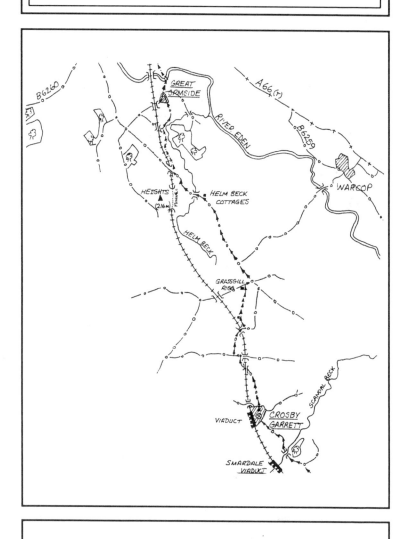

O.S. 1:50,000 Sheet 91. Appleby-in-Westmorland

left turn along a farm track leading to Grassgill Lodge. Some 200 metres from the lodge, the track turns sharply to the left and a footpath continues straight on to Grassgill Rigg. The path is found to be almost impassable, being greatly overgrown with all manner of plants, bushes and remains of trees. Having struggled through this morass of undergrowth, we again find our way blocked by an electric fence passing directly over the pathway.

Having overcome the difficulties of passage by Grassgill Lodge, it is a different story cutting through to Grassgill Rigg. Through the farmyard we are greeted by a pleasant wave and a cheery 'good morning' by the lady of the house, and higher up at Grassgill Rigg itself we are able to pass a few minutes of the day with Gordon Richards. No, not the Sir Gordon, he has been dead a few years now. Nor either the Gordon Richards who trains a large stable of chasers at Greystoke near Penrith. This is the Gordon Richards of Grassgill Rigg who used to train chasers but is now in semi-retirement, keeping only two horses with which he retains some interest in racing. Honest Jack is one of the pair. I must keep an eye out for it; I am sure it will be worth a pound each-way.

From Grassgill Rig we turn right to find a junction with the Soulby-Great Ormside road, at which point we turn left to suffer the hard metal for 2.5 kilometres until we reach the bridge over the line at Helm Cottage. Immediately before the bridge, the footpath leaves the road on the right and follows the line for a short distance before cutting over the fields and woodland towards Helm beck. We emerge from the pasture at the point where footpath, beck and lane to Great Ormside coincide, to find ourselves confronted by a lorry, a van and a gang of road menders putting the last touches of improvement to the country lane.

It is just a short 500 metre stretch into Great Ormside, a beautiful Eden Valley village. It is the sleeping kind you see in Sunday colour supplements and rarely seem to find when out looking for the same. But calamity, the troops are revolting again, no hostelry for the liquid refreshment so essential to the trekker's survival. I attempt to calm the angry mob with promises that this is the last place where no room will be found at an inn during our lunchtime halt. I am also desperately hoping that the brewers have not taken it upon their heads to close half the pubs in Cumbria. We decide to take a short rest break on the roadside verge. Ten minutes later the 'back-up'

GREAT ORMSIDE TO
LONG MARTON

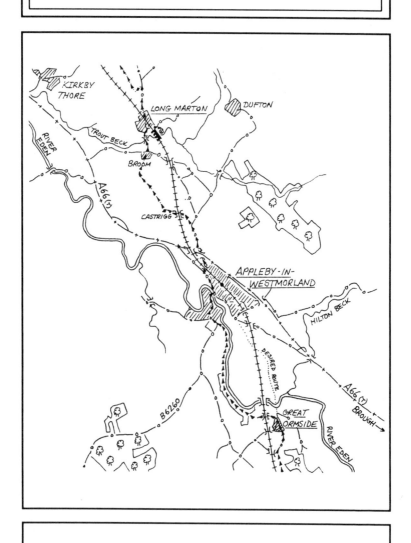

O.S. 1:50,000 Sheet 91. Appleby-in-Westmorland

team arrives unexpectedly as if by chance. And so it was! Mary and Alyson were on their way to retrieve the packs and though they would chance a visit to the village to ascertain progress. Having done so I go back to Crosby Garrett with Mary to pick up the packs. Arriving back in Great Ormside some half an hour later, we find Andrew still sound asleep where we left him, Ian carrying out treatment to his injured heel and Steve playing father with David and Kate. I forget where Alyson was.

Setting out from Great Ormside after the break, we make an error of navigation, or at least Andrew does. The desired route marked on the map follows the footpath out of the village at the north end, then proceeds to the east of the line, crossing the Eden and heading for Lowfield on the approach to Appleby. Unfortunately, Andrew chooses the pathway from the centre of the village, heading in a westerly direction, to pass under the line and follow a circuitous route round the river bank to arrive in Appleby via the Castle. Still, it turns out all right in the end, excepting the extra kilometre of foot-slogging on this now exceptionally hot first of June.

Arriving in Appleby at 2.45 pm, thoughts are directed towards some means of refreshment. Well, it is quite hot and we are all sweating in the afternoon sun. Having found a suitable inn, we partake of the local brew. Such is our concern to overcome the problems of dehydration that we forget completely the great sporting event of the day, the Derby, and fail to inflict grievous wallet harm to the local bookie with our £1 each way bets. As it turns out, Kahaysi wins and none of us would have backed it anyway. Following our couple of beers in the pub we turn our attention to food, finding a nice little cafe serving simple snacks just a few doors up the street. Sitting in the cafe devouring our first decent food since the evening before, the noise of people and traffic, the hustle and bustle of this lovely market town of Appleby, becomes noticeable for the first time. This is the first occasion we have experienced crowds and civilisation since leaving Settle three days before. The county town of now defunct Westmorland, Appleby on this day provides the visitor with a glimpse of what things used to be like, in those long-gone hot summer days that we all seem to remember but never seem to experience anymore. It's the bomb you know, or perhaps this new fangled 'greenhouse effect'.

Leaving the cafe after being nourished on pie, peas and

chips, we head out for the last four-kilometre stretch of the day. With a last look up the market place towards the castle, we turn north for Long Marton. Crowds of people still throng the walkways of the town centre, and as we cross the bridge over the Eden even more can be seen sitting, lying or playing along the broad grassy riverbank. Heading out of Appleby along the B6542, we pass the railway station, perched at the highest point in the town. The station itself is noted for the length of its platforms, one being a few centimetres short of 200 metres, and the fact that in the days of steam, water for the locomotives had to be pumped up from the Eden, some 50 metres below.

Further along the B6542, set back on the left, stands Appleby Grammar School, or at least that is what they called it way back in 1961 when I worked on the construction of the modern part of the school. Many happy memories flood back as we pass the place. Here is just one for the record. It was 8.20 on a Monday morning when the snow began to fall and at 8.40 it was standing exactly four inches deep on the bench top. I know because I was bringing the tools from their boxes in the cabin at the time and I measured it. The job was stopped that day, and did not open up again for over three weeks, due to snow, frost and ice. The brickies, joiners and labourers stayed at home, but Jack Fairs, a great old character, insisted that whilst we could do very little in the way of work, we had the duty to turn up on site ready to do so at the first opportunity. As it turned out we sat in our site cabin for the duration of the bad weather, wiling away the hours, playing cards or dominoes, or enhancing our education by reading the Daily Mirror.

A few metres past the school, we take a right turn under the railway bridge, leaving the B6542 to join the A66 trunk road for Penrith. This road leads to Dufton, a small village in which many a Pennine Way walker has made the overnight halt, gathering strength for the long march over Cross Fell to Alston. The road is also the place where for decades the gypsy horse traders have displayed their animals during the famous Appleby Fair. Following the road for only a few hundred metres, until it bears sharp right, we leave it at this corner to cross the fields to Castrigg which is to the west side of the line. We then join a made-up farm track to the small hamlet of Broom. The walking is very pleasant now in the warm sunshine, the fresh countryside at its best at this time of the year. A large herd of Friesian cattle occupies the fields around; there must be at least three hundred head.

Arriving in Broom, the roof tops of Long Marton can be seen less than a kilometre away. It may be only 600 metres but it seems like six thousand, yet it only takes a little over ten minutes. Thoughts of food and hot baths pass constantly through my mind as we tramp these last few metres. What kind of food doesn't seem to matter as long as it is hot and there is plenty of it, which, if I am any judge of Mary, there will certainly be. The simple pleasures of life are what spring to mind when one goes long-distance walking.

Up the slight gradient, round the bend to the village hall, fork back right on the road to Dufton, under the railway bridge, a few short metres and we are there. Today's journeys end is one short mile off the fifty. We pitch camp in the field in front of the cottage, courtesy of the farmer, who even tells us where the most even ground lies. The site is within 100 metres of Long Marton viaduct, where the Saturday before we had been lucky enough to see 4498 *Sir Nigel Gresley* hauling the Cumbrian Mountain Express out of Appleby to Carlisle. After completing the usual camp preparations we return to the cottage, each of us in turn to soak in a long hot bath before devouring an excellent meal, which was even more so in that it was prepared and cooked for us by Mary and Alyson. Slumped in chairs with our feet up afterwards, we relax our tired muscles and watch Kahyasi win the Derby. Where does a horse like that get the energy?

We retire to our tents at 11.00 pm that evening. Yes, Steve and I also, no sneaky cuddle-in's for us, having enjoyed a most perfect day.

LONG MARTON TO
CULGAITH

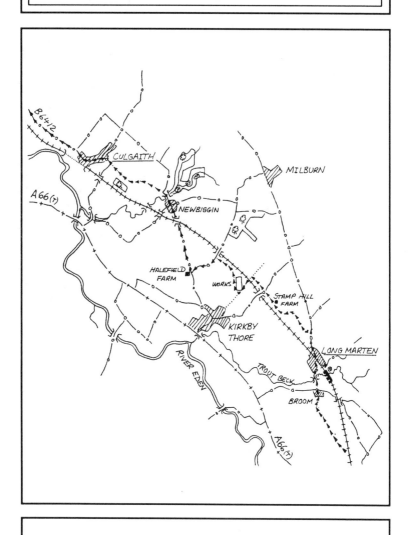

O.S. 1:50,000 Sheet 91. Appleby-in-Westmorland.

Chapter 5

Long Marton to Langwathby

"Four miles per hour yomp"

LEAVING Long Marton on the morning of our fifth day is none too easy. One quickly readjusts to the comforts of home and, whilst the night was spent under canvas, the luxury of sitting down to a full breakfast, sympathetically cooked by Mary and Alyson, occasions a less than enthusiastic effort to set out once again. The time is 10.30 before we eventually leave.

The brightness of sun and the clearness of the air quickly brush away any further feeling of sadness as we take the lane directly opposite the railway cottages at Long Marton, to head north along the eastern side of the line in the direction of Newbiggin. This lane is immediate first left under the railway bridge on the Long Marton-Dufton road

Some 250 metres on, the lane emerges on to the Long Marton-Milburn road, which we follow for a further 250 metres before taking the farm track on the left towards Stamp Hill Farm. The weather is perfect and the walking pleasant, with little hint of what is just around the corner. On reaching the end of the 'made-up' farm track, the footpath meanders over the meadow towards a bridge carrying the line over a small stream, just below Stamp hill Farm. Nowadays, this simple bridge has been promoted to a viaduct, as it also now straddles a large tube, approximately 1.3 metres in diameter, containing a conveyor belt. The material being conveyed is most probably gypsum for the plaster board factory close-by. Still, at least the tube is furnished with a stile at the point of the footpath. Negotiating the tube and stream we rise up the lane past Stamp Hill Farm to the Kirkby Thore-Milburn road. A short 'dog-leg' to the left and we take the lane on the opposite side of the road, immediately adjacent to the line some 15 metres below in a sharp cutting.

It is from this point that we have a first glimpse of the British Gypsum factory at Kirkby Thore. A scar on the Eden Valley landscape, the factory no doubt provides much needed employment in the area, and indeed a factory and gypsum mine have been a feature of these parts for many years past. As far back as 1906 gypsum was being transported by rail from the Newbiggin and Kirkby Thore sidings, when the company involved was known as T. McGhies. Not so far back, 1966 in fact, I worked many long hours in this self-same factory, installing pipeworks for the newly extended board mill. All around the factory and for many a square mile further, the creamy white dust settles on the leaves of trees, the bushes and the grass, and I wonder what it might do to the lungs of the people and animals who live and work around here?

The footpath from Stamp Hill approaches the factory on the east side of the line for some 300 metres, where it turns sharply left to cross the line at the southern end of the factory boundary, emerging on to the access road to the plant. The path we need to follow then turns northwards at a point where there now stands the factory gatehouse. Unfortunately the path then disappears from view, gobbled up by the encroaching tarmac of the factory approach road. With some trepidation we pass along this road, skirting the main buildings until we find ourselves moving into a desert of waste plaster and boards in a massive tip at the northern end of the plant.

It is with great relief that we leave the site behind when we pick up the pathway along a made-up lane at the northern end of the site just below the railway embankment east of Hale Grange. The road from Hale Grange Farm to Milburn is our next junction where we turn left, travelling eastward towards Halefield Farm. At this junction we turn right and north, heading for Newbiggin.

Approaching Newbiggin we pass under the line again by way of a now familiar brick-arched bridge, and proceed past a recently restored mill, now the workplace of a potter. The village sits at a crossroads, nestling in a valley bottom. The road to the left leads to Temple Sowerby, to the right once again there is Milburn, and straight ahead the road to Culgaith. Over the bridge of the Milburn Beck, the road takes us past Newbiggin Hall, up a steep incline of 1 in 7. Immediately at the point where the road turns back on itself in a rising reverse bend, the route carries forward along a made-up track towards Scar Top. The track continues to climb for about 100 metres, at which point it splits into a couple of footpaths, one heading to Scar Top, the other to Culgaith across the meadows. An accurate compass bearing is needed at this point in order to negotiate the field crossing so as to arrive at the lane end that takes the footpath into Culgaith. We do not take a bearing, and thus meander needlessly around field boundaries trying to relocate the footpath which is lost after passing over the first stile.

We arrive in Culgaith at 12.50, just in time for a good lunch in the Black Swan Inn, which is agreeably situated en route to Langwathby, our next destination and overnight stay. Lunch continues unabated for nearly two hours as we join a couple of visitors in a friendly game of pool.

Leaving the inn at 2.40 pm, we turn right on the B6412 for Langwathby. The road almost immediately bears right and picks up the route of the line at the point where it emerges from the northern mouth of Culgaith Tunnel alongside the River Eden. At 661 yards in length the third longest tunnel on the line, Culgaith was cut through the deep red sandstone of the Eden Valley. This is the same sandstone that produces such a marked contrast to the grey limestones of the Dales, wherever one sees any form of structure, be it house, farm, church or chapel.

Road, river and rail now travel together northwards, to within five miles of Carlisle, criss-crossing each other's paths via bridges, viaducts and tunnels, with little more than a couple of hundred metres between them. The stretch to Langwathby is approximately three-and-a-half miles, along a near straight road. My ankle and Ian's heel are still causing a great deal of pain, but once into a stride the pain appears to subside. With this in mind, and the thought that an early camp means a couple of hours rest before dinner, we set out on a fast march.

Four hundred metres on, the line disappears into the short Waste bank Tunnel, the site in 1930 of a head-on collision between a stationary ballast train and a northbound passenger train. The driver of the passenger train was killed and one of the passengers was later to die in hospital.

By the time we come abreast of Waste Bank Tunnel, our legs are in full swing and the pace is hotting-up. The sun is beating down and the sky is clear blue. The view all around is magic. To the west the Lakeland mountains, with the familiar saddle-back of Blencathra being easily identified. To the rear, fading now into the distance, the Howgills and Mallerstang. to the north, the Eden Valley, and well named it looks with every shade and hue of green to be seen. I had often reflected on what the latter part of the walk would be like, after we had left the hills behind. I need not have feared any boredom or

CULGAITH TO LANGWATHBY

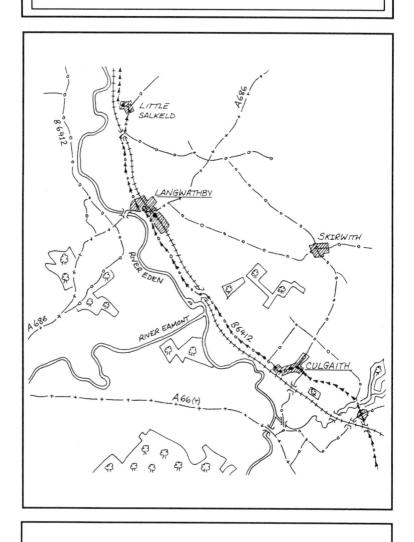

O.S. 1:50,000 Sheet 91. Appleby-in-Westmorland.

disinterest, as this country walking is every bit as exhilarating as our previous three days.

This idyllic setting is, momentarily, interrupted by two of those infernal low flying aircraft, skimming over the tree tops at what appears a dangerous height. Is it really necessary for this type of exercise to be conducted so close to people and animals, causing such disturbance to the way of life of the countryside?

The march picks up pace passing Moorside and then Staingills. The confluence of the rivers Eamont and the Eden is just below us, at a point where the road, river and railway come to within 100 metres of each other. The B6412 crosses over to the western side of the line at this point for the remainder of the trip into Langwathby. It is along this last stretch of road that we see coming towards us the two-car advance party on its way back to Long Marton. Mary and Alyson have delivered our packs into the hands of the local constabulary and also arranged that we might pitch in the garth to the rear of police station. At least we can sleep safe this evening!

Langwathby is a picturesque Cumbrian village, well worth a visit and a lovely place to stay. Our site for the night is once again within a few metres of the line, just below the embankment on a grassy knoll overlooking the village. The farm to which the field belongs is a hundred metres away. From it comes an entrepreneurial 10-year old who quickly provides us with half a dozen of the largest, freshest eggs I have ever seen. They will go down a treat at breakfast the following morning. A little while afterwards the same lad is back with a couple of pints of fresh milk. Later, we turn out for our evening meal at the Shepherdess Inn, the bill for four very nice bar meals and three sweets being extremely reasonable. It does not include the pints but we are most grateful for the hospitality just the same.

Turning in once again is a wet affair, as the rain begins to pour. Not that it is any inconvenience. There is something comforting about settling down into a sleeping bag under canvas (well nowadays it's nylon) to the soothing sound of rain rattling on the flysheet.

LANGWATHBY TO LAZONBY

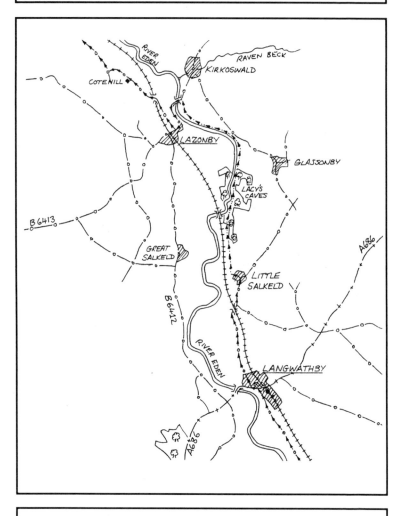

O.S. 1:50,000 Sheet 91. Appleby-in-Westmorland
O.S. 1:50,000 Sheet 90. Penrith & Keswick
O.S. 1:50,000 Sheet 86. Haltwhistle & Alston

Chapter 6

Langwathby to Armathwaite

"Delinquent Sheep"

WE are already two-and-a-half kilometres behind schedule when leaving Langwathby on the morning of Friday 3rd June. We had planned to rest overnight at Little Salkeld, but due to the lack of a suitable hostelry in this village, we thought it better to take the earlier 'stop-over'. Making up the extra two-and-a-half kilometres would not turn out too difficult, but at the moment of setting out it does not help the morale.

We take the 'B' road for Little Salkeld, at the fork in the village centre. The sky is overcast, but the cloud — remnant of last night's rain — is however beginning to break up and a nice day is promised. Immediately upon leaving Langwathby the line appears on the right, a matter of a few metres away. The Eden is clearly traced, less than a kilometre to the west, now beginning to flow along a much wider valley bottom than in the higher reaches.

About a kilometre out along the road to Little Salkeld, not far past the cemetary on the right-hand side, Ian finds he must answer the inevitable call of nature and disappears into a small copse on the roadside. Showing great concern for his welfare, we continue unabated in our relentless trek north. We do however take repeated glances over our shoulders to see if Ian is making up the leeway. Two hundred metres short of the point where the road drops to pass under the line adjacent to Little Salkeld station, I am pleased, looking over my shoulder, to see Ian, over a kilometre to the rear, still striding out in his inimitable fashion. He appears to be none the worse for wear. That however is the last we are to see of him for more than an hour. We continue down hill, under the bridge, past the station and on into Little Salkeld village, yet another little picture of rural beauty in the Eden Valley. The atmosphere of the place is set on its southern boundary by the restoration of the old mill, producing stone ground flour. The other parts of the village demonstrate fully the slow but steady pace of rural life anywhere.

We rest in the village centre for a short while before our thoughts return to our comrade Ian. The road at this point takes a sharp right hander for Gamlesby and the Gilderdale

LAZONBY TO ARMATHWAITE

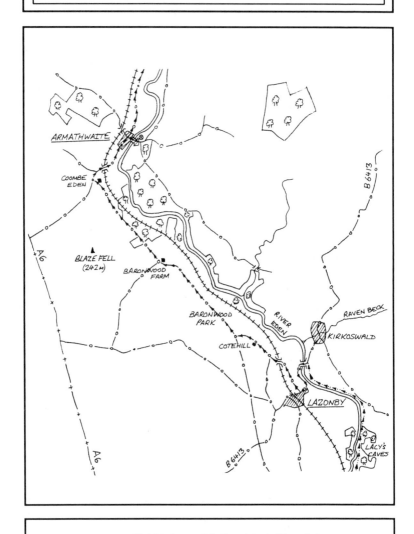

O.S. 1:50,000 Sheet 90. Penrith & Keswick
O.S. 1:50,000 Sheet 86. Haltwhistle & Alston

Forest, an area to which we had no intention of travelling. Andrew, being the youngest, fittest and therefore general factotum, is sent out on a reconnaissance mission to retrieve our wayward companion. More than half an hour later the two return. Ian had taken a sharp right as he came under the bridge at Little Salkeld station, deciding that the road to Melmerby was much more preferable to the planned route.

The team now up to full strength, we set off westward out of Little Salkeld on a made-up road that quickly turns northwards to run adjacent to the line in the direction of Lazonby. This road eventually becomes track and then cinder path as it makes its way towards the site of what was at one time Long Meg Sidings, in earlier days a major source of gypsum. The rails, sleepers and track equipment are now removed but the space, although overgrown, can still be readily identified. The line at this point runs from Little Salkeld to Long Meg in a cutting which has been the site of two strangely-related accidents. In 1918, engine No. 1010, hauling a St. Pancras to Glasgow express, ploughed into a landslide in the cutting, causing the death of seven passengers. Fifteen years later, in 1933, the same engine was pulling a Carlisle to St. Pancras train when it collided with a goods train. The driver of the goods train was killed. The coincidence of No. 1010 was not lost on enginemen, who afterwards feared to work the demon locomotive.

Passing through this spot, the well-defined track emerges from a wooded copse to overlook the impressive first crossing of the Eden by the Settle to Carlisle, over the Eden Lacy Viaduct. The pathway leaves the line at this point to follow the course of the Eden past Lacy's Caves, a well-known beauty spot of the Eden Valley, to emerge on to the B6143 Lazonby-Kirkoswald road just north of Lazonby village. As it is just after noon we seek refreshment in the village at the Joiners Arms. Very nice too!

It is upon leaving the inn after lunch that we, or should I say I, make our second mistake of the day. We leave Lazonby on a minor road, just to the west of the inn, that takes us past Lazonby Hall over Baronwood Park towards Baronwood Farm. Now the sight of numerous Highland cattle may do the heart of a countryman no end of good, but it did little for us, five and a half days out from Settle with only one and a half days to go. Much better I feel, the walk along the river bank through the Eden gorge and Baron Wood to Armathwaite. Still, decisions are made and consequences suffered. And the walking turned out to be quite pleasant if not a little boring. Well, Highland cattle are Highland cattle in Cumbria or Scotland.

The road continues over Baronwood Park and the side of Blaze Fell, in a near straight line for some seven kilometres, eventually meeting the High Hesket-Armathwaite road to Coombe Eden. This road then descends into Armathwaite, following the line on its eastern side. We have little difficulty in locating our packs as they are found holding a prominent place outside the local post office. Once again Mary and Alyson have done their job well. Finding a camp site for the night proves an easy matter, a local farmer offering an excellent pitch in a field on the east bank of the Eden. A further advantage of the site is the close proximity of the Fox and Pheasant Inn just over the field wall. Food and drink on the door step; that is if tents only had doorsteps. The site does prove to have a number of disadvantages, however, like a flock of sheep and a small herd of cattle. Not that we realise it at the time, but we are to do so during the course of the night.

Having rested for a couple of hours we go in search of stomach exercise in the hotel across the wall. Being Friday evening the lounge bar is extremely lively and we are made welcome by the locals. Well fed and watered, we leave at around 10.45 to return to base, only to find the tent that Andrew and I are using has been vandalised. A 90-degree tear, six inches long, is letting the light drizzle enter the front porch of the flysheet. An immediately search for the suspected delinquent is quickly called off when we realise that the culprit is none other than one of forty possible suspects. Interrogating thirty sheep and ten cows is not going to be easy. Images of a delinquent sheep on the loose in the heart of Cumbria promote nightmares during that night's restless sleep — restless due to the infernal bleating of these same animals for most of the night. Who ever suggested that a good idea to induce sleep was to count the damn things never went camping in Armathwaite.

Chapter 7

Armathwaite to Carlisle

"Race to the line"

WE leave Armathwaite at ten minutes past ten on the last day of our walk. The sun, once again shining, casts a pleasant early summer glow over the countryside. Expectant feelings of having completed the challenge are mixed with the knowledge that by mid afternoon our travels will be over and we will be going our separate ways. Whatever the difficulties we have encountered, particularly with injuries, we will remember the events of this journey for a long time to come.

The road leaves Armathwaite, heading north for Cumwhinton and Wetheral, following the line on the western side of the Eden. Two kilometres on we pass Dry Beck Viaduct, yet another example of the abilities of mid-Victorian railway engineers. At this point an alternative route, turning right down the track to Dry Beck farm and following a riverside path along the Eden to Duncowfold, is available. We decide, probably because of general fatigue, to continue along the road which does follow the path of the line more closely. The gradient begins to steepen, and within 700 metres the road bears sharply left, to cross the line at Low House crossing. The first drops of rain signal a heavy shower and the need to don cagouls for the first time since day one, during walking time.

Pressing on, the road leads past Wallace Field and Froddle Crook, where it then straightens for a long stretch to Duncowfold. Pounding the tarmac, we wish we had taken the more circuitous but lighter and more pleasant riverside path. Walking on grass is much more soothing to the feet. We continue along the road only as far as Shield Head where, as much as to give the feet some respite, we turn left down a path through Wetheral Shield. The footpath then passes over the line to approach Cumwhinton on the western side of the line. It is 12.10 pm, just in time for lunch. The Lowther Arms Inn stands on a fork in the roads leading to Harraby and Scotby, just off the B6263. We could see the pub from more than half a mile away. Half a mile is a terrible long way away from a pint of Jenning's when you are weary and dying of thirst. Eventually, after what seems an age, we stagger into the bar and slake our thirst.

ARMATHWAITE TO CUMWHINTON

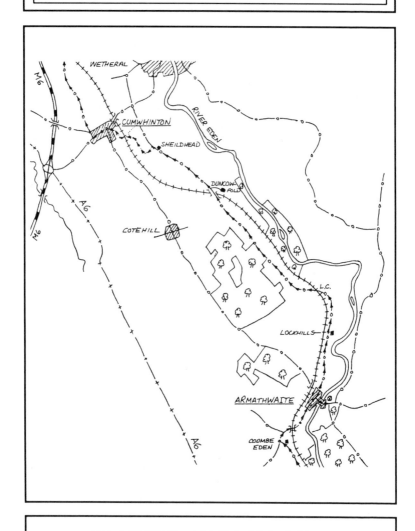

O.S. 1:50,000 Sheet 86. Haltwhistle & Alston
O.S. 1:50,000 Sheet 85. Carlisle & Solway Firth

Settled over pints of beer and thinking what we might have for lunch, it dawns on me that this is Saturday. Well, time seems so irrelevant when long-distance walking. But, being Saturday, it is the usual day for the steam excursions over the Settle to Carlisle. Thinking there may be a similar Cumbrian Express special today, as there had been the previous Saturday, I immediately ring Carlisle Citadel station to enquire. Yes, there is a special, the 'Gresley', 4498, leaving today at 12.45 pm, the same locomotive we had seen at Long Marton the week before. Ah! it is 12.40 already, and we are at least a kilometre from the line. For once the beer takes second place as, sore feet forgotten, we drain the last from our glasses and dash from the inn in a race to the line. The closest view point is along our route, the right-hand fork to Scotby from the inn. Three hundred metres further, a lane on the right runs down to the line still some distance away. Andrew is leading by some 200 metres at this point in a desperate bid to reach the railway and take photographs of the 'steamer'. Then some moments of disappointment as, still some distance from the line, we hear the whistle and then see the carriage roofs of a train running along a cutting just on the brow of the hill. Dejected, I stop to draw breath. Andrew is now some 300 metres away down the lane and across the fields, walking back towards the lane. I am joined by Ian and Steve.

Then we hear it, the distinct sound of a steam whistle. The train only two to three minutes earlier has been a false alarm; it was not the Cumbrian Mountain Express, hauled by *Sir Nigel Gresley,* at all. It is too late for us three to get to the railway now but Andrew immediately takes up the race again and heads for the line. He arrives in time to take some excellent shots while we stand back up the lane, watching the chimney and boiler top and coal-filled tender of 4498, followed by the carriage roofs of the train, wend their way through the meadows of the lower Eden valley on their way to Settle Junction. Reflecting afterwards, I felt it a pleasant turn of events that we had had the good fortune to see, on both the first and last day's of our journey, such an excellent example of the root cause of the journey, a steam locomotive beating its way along the Settle to Carlisle line.

Picking up our steps once again we return to the Cumwhinton to Scotby road at the top of the lane to be faced with a dilemma — how to negotiate a route which is now blocked by the M6 motorway? A northerly route through Scotby village is possible, but we take a left turn at Orchard House a kilometre on and

CUMWHINTON TO CARLISLE

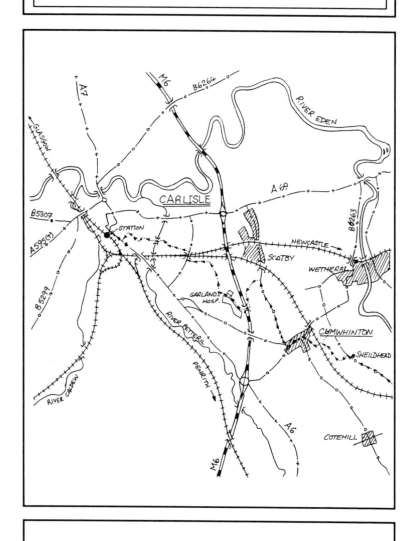

O.S. 1:50,000 Sheet 85. Carlisle & Solway Firth

follow the track until it forks. We bear left on the path heading southward until it eventually passes over the motorway to emerge adjacent to the Garlands Hospital. At the junction we turn right to head north again on a circuitous route around the hospital grounds. Two hundred metres past the church, we turn right along a side road that opens out on to open land that is crossed by an established pathway leading into the Harraby housing estate near a school. Continuing due north we pass through the streets of houses to emerge on to an open space along side the line. This same open space is the place where many years before I spent a great deal of my youth, playing soccer for Harraby United. Crossing the field, we turn left along the railway boundary until we reach the bridge carrying the A6-A69 link road over the line. We turn over the bridge and take the footpath down some steps into the Botcherby housing estate. The road directly opposite runs in a near straight line past the Metal Box factory to emerge on to an open space know as Melbourne Park, yet again the scene of many a 'Roy of the Rovers' drama thirty years ago.

Across the park and up through the streets of Botcherby in a north-westerly direction, we eventually meet the main road through Carlisle city centre, the A6. Bearing right up Botchergate, I have to admit to a feeling of great excitement and exhilaration, and a desire to turn the corner into Citadel Station square — journey's end. Two hundred metres can be a long way in such circumstances. Past the familiar shops, past the Caledonian Inn, the railwayman's pub, past the 'County' dance hall, finally turning the corner into the station square. We have arrived, seven days and 73 'rail' miles later, at the other end of the Settle to Carlisle railway line. The feet are sore and the legs weary, but the spirit is high, even if our outsides are not. Oh, I forgot to mention, we arrived in a thundering downpour.

Chapter 8

Alternative Routes

THE route as planned follows the Settle to Carlisle as closely as possible to the line itself. Use of footpaths and public rights-of-way is made wherever the opportunity arises, even if this means a short detour to avoid road walking. Even so, the need to resort to road and country lane walking is apparent from any study of the existing footways. It is hoped in due course, when the walk is more established, that the various authorities and interested parties involved may combine their resources to smooth out some of the irregularities and detours, thus providing a more accessible route alongside this most historic and beautiful of railways.

In the meantime some alternatives to the route described in this book are possible for the walker. Some of the alternatives are mearly minor deviations caused by the decision to follow one footpath as against another when planning the walk. Others are more difficult, due to the physical nature of the terrain and the absence of available footpaths or rights-of-way. The purpose of this chapter is to identify for the walker present and future alternative routes, leaving the final decision on which to follow to the individual. We feel that none of the alternatives listed detract from the pleasure of the walk, whilst some would positively add to it.

Helwith Bridge. A minor detour can be made here which is probably the more natural line of travel. Instead of taking the overgrown lane to the east side of the bridge, continue over the bridge towards Helwith Bridge village. Immediately after crossing the bridge, locate a footpath on the right-hand side of the road which heads northwards out of the village. One hundred metres on, take the right fork in the path, continuing northward to pass under the line in about 300 metres, to meet up with the original route at the footbridge over the Ribble, to the west of Studfold Farm.

Risehill Tunnel. One of the highlights of the Settle to Carlisle is the walk over the exact route of Blea Moor Tunnel, the longest on the line, by way of a well-defined footpath. Risehill Tunnel is second longest on the route, but no such footpath exists over this major structure. The walk from Dentdale to Garsdale is therefore somewhat marred by having to make a major detour along the old 'Coal Road'.

I feel certain that, with a little goodwill on behalf of all the authorities involved, a major enhancement of the walking route could be made by establishing a footpath over the direct route of Risehill Tunnel, as is the case with Blea Moor. The footpath could leave the Coal Road on the left, immediately adjacent to Dent station, and head north following the line towards Cowgill. The southern portal of Rise Hill Tunnel lies in pine forest owned by the Forestry Commission, and the tunnel emerges at the northern end on open moor above Garsdale. From here it is not inconceivable that a footpath may be laid along the lineside to Garsdale station, previously Hawes Junction, at Garsdale Head.

Moorcock-Ais Gill. Leave Yore House camp site via the entry lane to proceed north on the B6259 for Kirkby Stephen. In 300 metres, take the bridleway to the left, heading towards Grisedale by way of Moor Rigg. Close to the top of Moor Rigg the path turns north for Turner Hill and then on along the eastern lower slopes of Swarth Fell to descend to Ais Gill close by the cottages. From Ais Gill follow the footpath along the river bank until the route again joins the B6259. Cross over the road and the river by way of a footbridge and head for Deep Gill through Hazel Gill. Here the diversion meets up with the original route descending from the eastern slopes of Mallerstang Common.

Lazonby-Armathwaite. The locals reckon that the shortest route from Lazonby to Armathwaite is via Kirkoswald on the eastern side of the line and the river. if your preference is for local knowledge against the Ordnance Survey, then proceed out of Lazonby on the B6413. On reaching the village of Kirkoswald, fork left along an unmarked village road towards Staffield Hall. In about 300 metres, at the end of the housing, find a footpath on the left cutting across the fields to Staffield Hall. This path rejoins the road in about 1.5 kilometres, where a left turn will head one in the direction of Armathwaite. Follow the road as far as Combshead where a footpath can be found through the woodland eventually emerging on the east side of the river opposite Armathwaite Viaduct. A short walk along the riverside brings the traveller into Armathwaite and the welcoming sight of the Fox and Pheasant Inn.

A short but pleasant further diversion along this route takes the walker through the well-known local beauty spot of the Nunnery Walks. These walks can be found just after crossing

Croglin Water near Staffield Hall and are well worth the time and effort of a visit.

Cumwhinton-Harraby. After leaving Cumwhinton on the Scotby road and reaching the footpath at Orchard House, the path forks north and south. The northerly path is the more direct but the route to Harraby is blocked by the M6 motorway. The walk has then to backtrack a considerable distance to the south in order to pass under the motorway near Garlands Hospital. This diversion of over a kilometre could be overcome and a better 'desired line' produced if a footpath, properly fenced, could be allowed under the existing rail bridge, alongside the Settle to Carlisle. We appreciate the difficulties in doing so but the advantage gained would be to the enhancement of the walk and the enjoyment of many.

Long Marton railway cottages